THE NICENE CREED
FOR TODAY

THE NICENE CREED
FOR TODAY

BR. GREGORY SIMPSON

PARACLETE PRESS
Brewster, Massachusetts

Library of Congress Cataloging-in-Publication Data

Simpson, Gregory, 1938–
    The Nicene Creed for today / Gregory Simpson.
      p.   cm.
    ISBN 1-55725-236-X
    1. Nicene Creed. 2. Catholic Church—Doctrines.
I. Title.
BT999.S65   1999
238'.142—dc21
                          99-41516
                             CIP

10 9 8 7 6 5 4 3 2 1

© 1999 by The Community of Jesus, Inc.
ISBN 1-55725-236-X

Published by Paraclete Press
Brewster, Massachusetts
www.paraclete-press.com

Printed in the United States of America.

CONTENTS

PREFACE

In the Marketplace of Ideas

We live in a time of personal development. Office workers who used to spend their lunch hour in the cafeteria now spend it walking, jogging, or playing racquetball. Health clubs sponsor aerobic classes for young and old. Some people use free weights and "pump iron"; others choose Nautilus machines for their exercise. Swimming laps is popular, as are the martial arts of self-defense. People seek to manage their lives by reading books on stress relief, relaxation, goal setting, and treating oneself well. Many make a point of attending concerts and frequenting museums for intellectual and cultural enrichment. Self-improvement is now a way of life.

The same is true in matters of the spirit. New Age titles occupy the shelves of neighborhood bookstores. Angels have become the subject of books and television programs. Zen Buddhism and other Eastern religions find adherents among even those describing themselves as secular. While many are attracted by the "come as you are," "believe what you want" breadth of the New Age and similar movements, others long for clear truths and definitive answers to the questions that life poses. As a result, works on the Christian faith are becoming increasingly popular.

Christian leaders and churches that are often characterized as "conservative," with close ties to the Bible and the tradition of the church, offer explicit direction on morality and matters of faith and consequently are attracting new members. Many of the more "liberal" branches of the Christian church that do not provide specific guidelines for their constituents are struggling to maintain even their current levels of membership. Increasingly, however, more and more Americans want guidance for their faith and belief from sources independent of denominations and established hierarchies.

What to Believe

For those seeking wisdom and guidance about what to believe, especially within the Christian tradition, the question frequently asked today is "How can we know what to trust?" A lot of material on the market is written from a doctrinally slanted or proselytizing point of view.

Everyone knows that what we see advertised about a product is not always what we will get. We also know that groups advocating a cause may use biased language and may rearrange the facts to make their viewpoint appear attractive and worthy of support. It is even hard to find a newspaper whose news articles we can trust to be written without an editorial slant.

Knowing who authored the material, however, helps to gauge the truthfulness of what we read. It has been said that God neither deceives nor can be deceived, and it has always been the faith of the Christian tradition that certain documents are trustworthy because they have been inspired by the Spirit of God. One paramount example is the Holy Bible. Others are the statements issued by any of the seven ecumenical councils convened between AD 325 and 787, during the centuries of the early church before there were denominations as such. One such statement is the Nicene Creed, which since AD 325 has helped to define Christian theology and has been an element common in almost all Christian worship. Although of ancient formulation (actually composed between AD 325 and 451), this brief declaration has circumscribed theological discourse since its formulation and has provided the earnest seeker with enduring truths about God and the church.

How to Believe

Before approaching the Nicene Creed, however, we should take a quick look at faith itself. The pursuit of faith is one each individual must make. The real motive for faith comes from within, since faith is by free assent only. Nothing can force faith, and nothing can destroy it. Real belief is always in one's own. The heart, an unassailable fortress, is unlocked only from within.

Why do some find it easy to believe, and others have difficulty? One critical factor is the person's attitude. If God, or material about him, is enterend into with openness, the likelihood of acceptance is greater. If one has a skeptical, "show me" stance, receiving unprovable material into one's heart will be much harder.

Since no one can coerce another to believe, a person's disposition is important.

The church has taught that searchers for the truth have two things working in their behalf. One is the gift of faith that God gives to those who search. Those pursuing him are enabled by his grace to affirm what they might otherwise find beyond their ability to accept. The second is the great company of the faithful; those seeking faith do not do so in isolation. As we have not given ourselves life, so we do not give ourselves faith.

One American ideal, which we have inherited from the pioneer years of this country's settlement, is that of the lone frontiersman, traveling westward to conquer the unknown and carrying only those earthly goods that were portable. Such steadfast individualism was requisite for those establishing a new nation. Those who followed, however, needed a sense of community and stability. Rather than always looking to the horizon, these folk had to depend on one another and settle down in the place where they were living. They were part of a network that cooperated to establish a way of life, interdependent and supportive. Most believers are settlers. Each is a link in a blessed chain of faithful souls. Many find themselves in communities of faith, where it is easier to believe. In a faithful community one can find encouragement, and the good of one is the good of all.

What we know about God is also the fruit of a communal undertaking. Our knowledge of him was not concocted in this generation, but handed down from the past and from humanity's contemplation of matters eternal. It is our inheritance from the early centuries when men and women laid down their lives, preferring martyrdom to betrayal of the truths about God they held dear. In later years theologians fashioned Christian doctrine on the anvil of public debate. There is now a great treasure of truths about God and his dealings with the world that have been entrusted to us. A part of this treasure is the Nicene Creed.

Faith and Reason in Studying a Creed

One useful tool in the search for faith is reason. Reason, however, does not lead us inevitably to faith. Belief is not found at the end of a syllogism. Reason can guide the inquirer to the edge of the precipice. Faith is not a leap we take in the dark, but a leap from the darkness into the light. The choice to jump, however, is up to the individual.

To use a different picture, reason can be likened to the headlights of a car traveling by night on an unknown road. The lights provide illumination for the trip—turns in the road, potential exits from the route, obstacles that may lie across the way. According to what the headlights reveal, the driver makes decisions whether to turn, stop, speed up, or change direction. In similar fashion the intellect can guide the inquirer through a potential article of faith. While we cannot follow reason into faith, we can use it to be sure that what we believe makes sense and has validity for us.

It is interesting to note that like reason, the supernatural does not necessarily produce faith. Many witnessed the miracles of Jesus, but only some believed. The preaching of Paul wrought many conversions, but not in the hearts of everyone. So great a wonder as the Resurrection did not automatically elicit faith—even among the disciples who knew and loved Christ. Faith, therefore, is not an inevitable and mechanical result of either arguments or evidence.

Faith is finally the complete giving of oneself to God, not just to the truths and creeds about him. A seminal theologian of the church, Thomas Aquinas (1225–1274), once remarked wisely that our faith should not end in the propositions, but in the realities themselves. Faith is, first and foremost, personal adherence to God. The creeds and other statements about him are the glasses through which we can view him more clearly, but if they are handled and examined for their sake alone, the fingerprints left on those lenses will obscure the One whom they were designed to enable us to behold.

It is the hope of the author of these meditations that those engaged in an initial search for Christian faith, as well as veteran believers desiring more insight into the nature of God, may discover what countless people before us have found—that the Nicene Creed, a central core of the faith that preceded all divisions that divide the church, is a fascinating and trustworthy deposit of truth for seekers of all ages.

one

THE LINE DRAWN
IN THE SAND

To begin the story of the Nicene Creed, we must to go back sixteen centuries to a time of turmoil and unrest in the Christian church. With the dawn of the fourth century, faith in the risen Christ had spread throughout the Mediterranean world. Missionaries and soldiers, merchants and travelers had taken the news of the risen Messiah to every corner of the Roman Empire. As the message spread, it encountered cultures and languages alien to the Jewish milieu in which Jesus and his followers had lived and the church had begun. Of these cultures, the most influential was that of the Greeks. Hellenism (from the Greek word for "Greek") dominated the part of the world where the church was expanding.

Hellenistic philosophy had a long and well established way of describing God and God's relationship with creation. The supreme deity was completely above and separate from creation, totally unique and transcendent. God was pure spirit at the highest and purest level of the orders of reality. At the lowest level of reality was pure matter, dark and devoid of life and truth.

Between these two extremes of the cosmos existed myriad aeons, or levels of being. Those closest to God participated in his pure being with just the smallest degree of matter in their makeup. Conversely, those closest to matter were composed mostly of matter, with just a hint of spirit within. Each level mediated the one above to the one below and the one below to the one above, so that through these intermediary layers the most high God was eventually present to earth. In God's exalted state existed an indivisible nature, God possessing neither passions nor transformations. God was perfect. No sentence could be uttered in Hellenistic circles with *God* as the subject and *change* as the verb.

We can therefore understand that when people with this outlook first heard the allegation that the most supreme God had personally come to earth—the domain of that basest substance, matter—they were confused and incredulous. The supreme God become matter? Inconceivable. Spirit commune with matter? Absurd.

All manner of schemes arose to explain the unexplainable. The controversy that swirled around the attempts to make sense of the insensible embroiled the Roman Empire and its new emperor, Constantine, in a controversy that took two major church councils and many decades to conclude—and while the doctrines in question have long since been settled, the ideas outlawed in the fourth-century conflict are still found throughout the church. The fire and energy with which this fight raged are difficult for us to appreciate: Matters that elicit little more than a shrug today were causes for which many suffered, and for which some preferred going to the stake rather than betray the beliefs they held so dear.

The questions that faced the church were these: "Who is Jesus Christ?" and "What is his relationship with God the Father?" Old truths had to be cast in new molds. Two groups formed in the acrimonious debate that ensued: those who followed Arius, a priest from Alexandria, and those who were ranked against him.

The Popularity of Arius

Alexandria was the second city of the Roman Empire, a center of Hellenistic thought and the location of a famous school dedicated to the spread of Christianity among the more cultured classes.

4

Arius's contemporaries described him as tall and handsome, leading an ascetic lifestyle, earnestly religious, and an eloquent preacher in the influential Baucalis Church. Although he became the head of the exegetical school of that city, his ideas about Christ and the movement that he began were more influential and memorable than the man himself.

Arius can be described anachronistically as a thoroughgoing Unitarian. He held that there is but one God, the God of the Old Testament and the God of Jesus Christ. This being is absolutely transcendent and perfect, and there can be no other God beside him. He believed that direct contact between God and creation would annihilate all of created reality, so different are they in being. God, however, is a God of love, and he wanted to rescue humanity from the sin and darkness into which they were plunged when Adam and Eve sinned against him in the Garden of Eden. He created a Son, who alone can mediate salvation. Arius could call him the "Son of

God," as the church had always done, but his interpretation of the term caused a revolution. For him, Jesus *grew* into his sonship by unfailing obedience to the Father. Because of this, God adopted him as his son. Although a Son of a much higher degree than we, he, like us, was adopted into the family of God's children.

Unlike the eternal God, Arius said, the Son had a beginning. What John declares in his Gospel, that "all things came into being through him" (John 1:3), is true, but Christ is the Son *of* God, brought into being by God out of nothing. "There was a time when he was not," is how Arius phrased it. Christ is the highest and best of the created order, first in time and degree. He could not be God, however, because there are only Creator and created, and he was not the Creator. This subordinate being suffered and died, always in worship and adoration of the Father who had sent him. Such a concept of Jesus was a perfect Hellenistic expression of the gospel.

6

As Arius stated in a letter to Alexander, his bishop:

> We acknowledge one God, alone unbegotten, alone everlasting, alone unbegun, alone true, alone having immortality, alone wise, alone good, alone sovereign: judge, governor, and administrator of all, unalterable and unchangeable, just and good, God of law and prophets and New Testament; who begat an only-begotten son before eternal times, through whom he has made both the ages and the universe. . . .

The recipient of this statement was the bishop of Alexandria, the bishop to whom Arius was responsible. No love was lost between the two men, however. Alexander recognized the implications of his priest's ideas and went to great lengths to quash an increasingly popular movement.

Arius wrote to Eusebius, who had studied under the same teacher as he and who was now bishop of Nicomedia:

> I want to tell you that the Bishop [of Alexandria, Alexander] makes great havoc of us and persecutes us severely, and is in full sail against us; he has driven us out of the city as atheists because we do not concur in what he publicly preaches, namely, that "God has always been, and the Son has always been. . . ." We are persecuted because we say "the Son had a beginning, but God is without beginning." This is really the cause of our persecution, and, likewise, because we say that he is from nothing. And this we say because he is part neither of God, nor of a lower essence.

All contenders in this great Christological debate—those in Arius's camp and those opposed to him—made continual appeal to two great standards of truth: the Scriptures and salvation. If an idea could be grounded in the Bible, or at least shown that it did not contradict it, that notion would meet the first criterion of truth. The second was what is necessary for salvation. If an argument could be made that such-and-such is required for God to save humanity, then it would meet this standard of truth.

Arius found many verses in the Bible to show that the Son is inferior to the Father. The human characteristics of Christ proved to Arius that the Son was less than the real God. Was Jesus not born of a woman under Jewish law? Did he not pray to the Father, suffer the bodily weaknesses of hunger, thirst (John 19:28), and fatigue (John 4:6), and show his fear in Gethsemane (Mark 14:32–36)? None of these would the true God endure. And he was crucified. Among his final words was a cry of desperation from the cross: "My God, my God, why have you forsaken me?" (Matt.

27:46). He experienced growth in wisdom (Luke 2:40) and asked questions (Matt. 16:13), plainly revealing his ignorance. Jesus himself admitted that his Father knew more than he: "But about that day or hour no one knows, neither the angels in heaven, nor the Son, but only the Father" (Mark 13:32). Even his words are not original: "I have not spoken on my own, but the Father who sent me has himself given me a commandment about what to say and what to speak" (John 12:49). He identified with the rest of humanity in its subordination to God, describing the Father as "My God and your God," (John 20:17), and he said to his disciples, "The Father is greater than I" (John 14:28). Even after the resurrection, Peter places Christ as the object of his Father's actions: "God has made [Jesus] both Lord and Messiah" (Acts 2:36), as did Jesus before he died, describing himself as "the one whom the Father has sanctified and sent into the world" (John 10:36). Arius and his friends could cite as well the statements from Jesus' own lips: "I can do nothing on my own" (John 5:30), and from Mark, "Why do you call me good? No one is good but God alone" (Mark 10:18).

Not only from Scripture, but from philosophy as well, was it clear to the Arians that the Son was not equal to the Father. They were of two different natures, the one Creator, the other created, and so a radical gulf separated them, making a close and intimate relationship between them impossible. In the Hellenistic view they belonged to two different planes of existence, so the Son could have no direct, genuine knowledge of his Father.

The Son might be called by divine names, as he is in the Bible, but only as a courtesy, so to speak. At the heart of the Arian gospel was a Savior who had suffered and died. They therefore took the incarnation very seriously. Because the God they knew was immune to both harm and death, a God of a lesser divinity was necessary—one who was divine, but who could experience the suffering aspect of saving humanity. The scandal of the cross was much sharper in the Arian camp than in the other. Such a focus was achieved, however, at the expense of their doctrine of God. There were two divine beings, a high God, incapable of suffering, and a lower God, who, as one writer put it, did the dirty work of the first.

Arius had particular ideas, not only about the Son's relationship with the Father, but also about the makeup of Christ. His view of human nature was derived from Plato's, who said that humans are matter (the body) animated by a soul (spirit). In the Gospel of John, Arius found material that was easily interpreted in this light: "In the beginning was the Word, and the Word was with God, and the Word was God. And the Word became flesh and lived among us, and we have seen his glory, the glory as of a father's only son, full of grace and truth" (John 1:1, 14). In the Hellenistic

12

scheme, the Word *(or Logos)* was an aeon just below the high God, a kind of organizing principle that brought order to the chaos of matter. Arius said that when the Word became flesh, it took the place of the soul in the human Jesus. A mere human could not save humanity; only a divine being would have that power. The Son of God could be spoken of as divine, since the animating principle of his whole person, his soul, was divine.

It is easy to see why Arius had such a following, since everything he said about the Father and the Son fit so well into the thought of the day. He made up clever ditties expressing his ideas and had the dockhands singing them as they worked around the port of Alexandria. His views appealed especially to recent converts, whose childhood paganism knew of a supreme God who made lesser gods that passed back and forth between heaven and earth to do his work.

The Anti-Arian School

It was not only his bishop (Alexander) who fought Arius, but also a large contingent of churchmen who were alarmed by both his ideas and his popularity. One such man was Athanasius, who became a stalwart defender of the faith in the controversy that swirled around Arius and his ideas.

Born about AD 300 of upper-class parents, Athanasius showed a deep interest in the church from early childhood. Alexander took early notice of him and brought him under his wing. He was of stalwart character, keen insight, and a deep religious faith. Courageous to a fault, he successfully opposed the Emperor Constantine on two different occasions and defied the emperor's son, Constantius, either openly or secretly for most of his career. When he had it in his power to do so, he denied Arius and his followers a place to worship in the city. He openly declared his hatred for both Jews and Arians.

Athanasius had his dark side. A number of the statements he made have been proved to be outright lies, calculated to shore up his own positions and cast his opponents in a bad light. One of his favorite targets was the Meletians, followers of one Meletius, who had started his own church by ordaining some fellow bishops and attracting a respectable number of followers. In papyri discovered at the beginning of this century were found two letters detailing how Athanasius mistreated the Meletians. One was written by Callistus, a Meletian monk or priest, who made these claims:

> [Athanasius] arrested the [Meletian] bishop of the lower country and shut him up in the meat market, and he shut up a presbyter of those parts also in the lockup, and a deacon in the great prison, and Herascius [apparently an eminent Meletian bishop] has been imprisoned since the 28th in the camp. I

thank the Lord God that the beatings which he was receiving have ceased. And on the 27th [Athanasius] forced seven bishops to leave the area.[1]

Eventually formal charges were brought against Athanasius at the Council of Tyre by another bishop, Eusebius of Caesarea. These included causing divisions and disturbances in his diocese, preventing people from entering churches to pray and worship, imprisoning people, beating people undeservedly, and burning churches. He was even charged with murder. Apparently there is little reason to doubt the validity of many of these accusations. He managed to weather these storms of allegation, however, and with his advancing years came wisdom and his development into a statesmanlike figure.

This Athanasius was the main spokesman for those arrayed against Arius. He had a threefold critique of his opponent's view of Christ. The first was that Arius's description of the Trinity undermined it by inhabiting the Godhead with three different kinds of gods—a supreme Deity and two lesser divinities, creating a polytheism wholly alien to the Judeo-Christian tradition. For their part, Arians claimed their opposition confused the distinct Persons of the Trinity by blending the distinct characteristics of each. In their view, of course, with no common nature shared among them, there was no chance of mistaking their particularity.

Athanasius appealed, in the second place, to the liturgical tradition of the church. He cited the formula used in baptism—"in the Name of the Father, the Son, and the Holy Spirit"—as clearly implying equality among the three members of the Trinity.

His final argument dealt with what is necessary for salvation. He agreed with Arius's assertion that the Mediator must be divine to restore the relationship between God and the world. He pointed out, however, that Arius's Christ was not as much God as the Father was, maintaining that it is only a divinity of the fullest stature that could effect salvation.

He was also fond of citing verses of Scripture that show the Son has always been God. The Gospel of John was his favorite book for these proofs. Did not the evangelist state that "In the beginning was the Word, and the Word was with God, and the Word was God. He was in the beginning with God. All things came into being through him, and without him not one thing came into being" (John 1:1–3)? He called Mary "the God-bearer," recollecting another verse from John: "And the Word became flesh and lived among us, and we have seen his glory, the glory as of a father's only son, full of grace and truth" (1:14).

He noted that Paul continues in this vein in his letter to the Philippians: "[Christ, who] was in the form of God, did not regard equality with God as something to be exploited, but emptied himself, taking the form of a slave, being born in human likeness. And being found in human form, he humbled himself and became obedient to the point of death—even death on a cross" (2:6–8). He saw a clear reference to the full divinity of the Son in Matthew's quote from Isaiah's prophecy: "'Look, the virgin shall conceive and bear a son, and they shall name him Emmanuel,' which means, 'God is with us'" (1:23).

Athanasius denied that the fact Christ "received" things from the Father proves his inferiority: ". . . [The Son] did not receive any of the things he says he received without already possessing them, for the Logos possessed them eternally as God. It is in virtue of his being human that we now say 'he received,' with a view to asserting that . . . the flesh was, in him, the recipient."

What about the nature of Christ? Athanasius viewed the Logos as eternally divine. While resident in the man Jesus, he remained omnipotent, running the entire universe as he had before the incarnation. Not only did the Logos remain divine, but Jesus remained wholly human, retaining all of his faculties, including that of his soul. Christ had both a divine and a human nature. This was essential to salvation. It is Christ's body, they argued, that saves our body, and his soul that saves our soul. Without complete humanity, God's Son could never be a complete Savior. Athanasius stated his position clearly: "If the work of the Logos' Godhead had not been done by means of the body, humanity would not have been divinized. Furthermore, if the properties of the flesh had not been reckoned to the Logos, humanity would not have been completely liberated from them."

He also makes the point that the Word did not just enter a human being (as Arius and his companions claimed), but actually *became* human:

[The Logos] became human. He did not enter into a human being. It is, moreover, crucial to recognize this. Otherwise, . . . [people] might suppose that just as in earlier times the Logos "came to be" in each of the saints, so even now he came into residence in a human being, sanctifying this one also and being revealed just as he was in the others. If this were the way of it, and all he did was to appear in a human being, there would have been nothing extraordinary, nor would those who saw him have been astonished and said, "Where does this man come from?" (Mark 4:41) and "Why do you, who are a human being, make yourself God?" (John 10:33), for since they heard the expression "and the word of the Lord came to" each of the prophets, they had some acquaintance with the idea. . . . It is said that he took on flesh and became a human being and suffered on our account in that flesh. . . . The purpose of this was to demonstrate and to bring all to believe that, although he is always God, . . . in the end and on our account he became a human being, and "the Godhead dwelt bodily" (Col. 2:9), as the apostle says, in the flesh. This amounts to saying, "Being God, he had his own body, and using this as an instrument, he became a human being on our account." (*Orations against the Arians*, Book III)[2]

An Evaluation of the Conflict

We know the judgment of history and the church: Arius was declared a heretic; Athanasius and his group prevailed. Before tracing how this came to pass, two observations are worth noting.

The first is a critique of the Arian Christ. Neither wholly human nor wholly divine, he is as remote from humanity as he is from God. Since he does not partake of the complete nature and power of God, he cannot in any real way be described as the Son of God, nor as the divine Word. Arius and his followers had cast the biblical Jesus into a philosophic mold, rather than using philosophy to express the gospel truths about Christ.

Something must also be said about the nature of the conflict. Both the Arians and their opponents sought to promote their respective views as if they had always been in the church's tradition and were securely buttressed by Holy Scripture. Both sides cast the other as outside the pale of orthodoxy. Such was not the case, however. There was no "orthodoxy" on the subject of the person of Christ. That is what they were working out. These years of controversy involved seekers of good faith, from across the theological spectrum, engaged in a quest for the truth. Bishops were called upon to bear testimony; riots took place; vitriol was not spared by either side; and an ancient schism between the Latin-speaking West and the Greek-speaking East, predating the church, widened into a breach that endures to this day. Had the issues been clear, and the division between right and wrong doctrine well defined, the controversy would not have raged on for more than sixty years, involving several Roman emperors and some twenty councils. It is to this account that we now turn.

two

NICAEA— ARENA OF THE CONFLICT

Emperor Constantine had a problem. Now the sole ruler of the Roman Empire, he wanted to consolidate his power and unify his newly won empire. He had recently embraced the faith of the Christian church, and it was his hope that the church would be the catalyst for unity. It was this very church, however, divided over what seemed to him a minor theological matter, that was threatening to tear his realm in two.

The controversy had started as a purely local quarrel between Alexander, the bishop of Alexandria, and Arius, one of his priests, over the matters discussed in the previous chapter. What began as a regional conflict soon spread. Arius enlisted influential support from outside Egypt—men such as Eusebius of Caesarea (located on the seacoast of Palestine), the most learned figure of his age, and another Eusebius, the bishop of Nicomedia (a seaport in northwest Turkey).

Alexander, for his part, summoned his episcopal colleagues into council to examine Arius's beliefs. He placed a confession of orthodoxy in front of his rebellious presbyter with the demand that he sign it. When Arius refused, Alexander excommunicated both him and a number of the bishops who supported his cause. He sent a letter to many of his bishops warning them about both Arius and Eusebius of Nicomedia.

In a countermove that widened still further the division in the church, in Palestine a council was convened that declared Arius's views orthodox and demanded that Alexander reinstate him.

Indeed, the emperor had a problem.

Constantine drafted a letter to both Alexander and Arius and sent it by his trusted aide, Hosius, a bishop of Cordova in southern Spain. In the letter the emperor ordered them to settle their conflict forthwith and mutually to forgive one another. He stated that after "careful inquiry into the origin and foundation of these differences [he found] the cause to be of a truly insignificant character and quite unworthy of such fierce contention." He further charged them to hold their discussions "merely as an intellectual exercise . . . and not hastily produced in the popular assemblies, nor unadvisedly entrusted to the general ear."

The Emperor's view of the debate's insignificance was shared by many of the faithful. One Christian who had suffered in the recent persecutions later told the debaters at Nicaea that Christ did not "teach us dialectics, art, or vain subtleties, but simplemindedness, which is preserved by faith and good works." Despite the

27

emperor's letter, a quiet settlement of the matter was not forthcoming. His appeal fell on deaf ears.

The parties were unwilling to yield in their positions. An outside force was needed to effect a settlement. At this point, Constantine's courier, Bishop Hosius, stepped into the spotlight. He knew what the wrath of a ruler could do, having suffered under the persecution of Maximian, one of Constantine's predecessors. Whether motivated or not by this terrible memory, he forsook his role as mailman and entered the fray on the side of Alexander. Early in 325 he traveled to Antioch to preside over a church council that excommunicated Arius's supporter Eusebius of Caesarea.

At this point the emperor himself took charge of matters, perhaps inspired by a report Hosius had written him. He chose a precedent-setting course by convening a churchwide council for the settlement of major church disputes. Hosius himself was to take part in the momentous events that followed. He would live to be a century old and serve the church both in exile and as bishop until his death. Constantine appropriated a council already scheduled for later that year in Ancyra (modern Ankara, the capital of Turkey), moving the council to Nicaea, a little town near the Sea of Marmara located closer than Ancyra to his residence in Nicomedia. He may have done this to stay on top of the proceedings, because he was shocked that any party, like the anti-Arian contingent that had dominated the council Hosius chaired, could excommunicate as respected a theologian as Eusebius. He also may have had in mind his inability to settle another church controversy in northern Africa, one where he had not been personally present to exert his imperial influence.

Last-minute informal discussions between the Arians and their opponents held before the opening of the Council produced no agreements. Despite the Council's significance in the history of

Christian thought, there are no detailed records of what transpired there, although we are able to piece together some of the Council's actions through informal sources that were preserved, one of which is Eusebius of Caesarea's *Life of Constantine*.[3] Of official documents, we have the creed the Council produced, a letter they drew up, and twenty canons they approved.

The number of bishops present is not known, because the lists of signatures we possess are not reliable. Athanasius reported that there were 318 episcopal representatives in attendance, but this may be a symbolic figure based on the number of servants Abraham is said to have had: "When [Abraham] heard that his nephew had been taken captive, he led forth his trained men, born in his house, three hundred eighteen of them, and went in pursuit as far as Dan" (Gen. 14:14). The Council became known by that number as "the Synod of the 318 Fathers." It is now thought that 200 to 250 is the more likely number, most of them coming from the neighboring eastern part of the empire, with all expenses paid from the imperial treasury. Despite his importance in the whole church, the bishop of far-off Rome could not attend because of his age, so two priests represented him. The only other delegates from the West were Hosius; the bishops of Carthage, Milan, and Dijon; and two other unnamed men. Hundreds of lesser clergy and lay people also attended.

The Council began in May 325. At its opening, Emperor Constantine made his entrance before the assembled bishops arrayed in a majestic robe of ornamented silk, leaving no doubt about who was in charge. His entrance may have shaken some of those present, not a few of whom bore the marks of lashings ordered by previous emperors. An Egyptian pastor present was missing an eye, and another arrived crippled in both feet because of torture by branding irons.

Constantine spoke only briefly, saying that it was imperative they come to some settlement of the dispute rending the church. "Division in the church is worse than war," he declared. While his passion was political, not theological, he made it clear that he deplored the censure of Eusebius of Caesarea, by whom he had been lavishly praised; Constantine even declared full support for his doctrine.

After the emperor's remarks, the disputants were allowed to present their arguments. A violent controversy ensued, even though most present had not made up their minds. On the one hand, there were Arius and his supporters, vocal and persuasive; on the other, an equally determined faction led by Alexander. One of the latter's followers was Athanasius, at that time a deacon, a young churchman destined to became a champion of orthodoxy.

The Arians were the first to present their views. They did so in the form of a creed submitted by Eusebius of Nicomedia, but it was quickly and soundly rejected by the council.

The other Eusebius (of Caesarea) was apparently the next to volunteer. An early supporter of Arius, he was universally acknowledged as the most scholarly bishop of his day, and one with whom neither side could find fault. Although he supported Arius, he cannot be categorized as a wholehearted Arian, since by personal bent he was a historian and antiquarian, and only by the exigencies of his office was he a bishop, and a theologian. He was one of many who of necessity had been forced to become acquainted with the theological issues engulfing the church. Although not an eloquent author—his style is vague and affected—at his death he left a large number of literary works.

Born about the year 264, Eusebius began his career of study before being ordained a priest in his twenty-fourth year. Twenty-three years later he was made bishop of Caesarea and would henceforth be involved in church politics until his death at age 75. He viewed

Christ in ways similar to those of Arius, declaring him to be a creature, having been made by the Father, who alone is eternal. How this took place, he said, is beyond human understanding because God is outside human comprehension. Like many of his contemporaries, he applied Proverbs 8:22 to the Son: "The LORD created me at the beginning of his work, the first of his acts of long ago." God is a completely unknowable and abstract first power, he wrote. There exists also the Logos, or organizing principle, with the ability to take form and reveal this higher principle. Perhaps strangest of all to our modern ears is his notion, shared by others of his century, that Christ's physical body at the end of time would be absorbed into the life of the higher God and disappear. Jesus was the one "born according to the flesh, which stood in succession from David, which Christ used when he was in it."

Many people of Arius's day had an undeveloped view of the Holy Spirit, and

Eusebius was no exception. He saw the third Person of the Trinity as much less than the Father or the Son, more like a ministering spirit who is not divine, yet greater than humans or angels.

Eusebius submitted a creed which he had used in Caesarea to teach those who wanted to become Christians, and which they recited at their baptism. The bishops and the emperor embraced this creed, hoping it might be the long-sought compromise that would serve to unite the strife-torn church. For some reason, long since lost to history, it was never chosen by the Council as the final creed, despite its initial approval.

From a philosophically worded statement, the bishops turned next to creeds containing only terms from the Bible. Using scriptural terminology alone, however, they were unable to strictly exclude Arius's doctrines. The bishops who sympathized with Arius were reported to be winking and nodding to one another that, following the Council's adjournment, they would be able to interpret any such document and make it agree with their position. Finally another proposal was submitted by an anonymous author from the area of Palestine. Accepted by the assembly as being watertight against Arian misinterpretations of Christ's nature, it was issued as the official creed of the Council.

A comparison of this with Eusebius's document illustrates not only the differing views of the two parties, but also clarifies two Greek terms that have helped define the faith of the church.

The Creed Eusebius Submitted

We believe in one God, the Father Almighty, maker of all things, visible and invisible,
> and in one Lord Jesus Christ,
> the word [*Logos*] of God,
> God from God,
> light from light,
> life from life,

The Creed the Council Accepted

We believe in one God, the Father Almighty, maker of all things visible and invisible,

and in one Lord Jesus Christ,
the Son of God,

the only-begotten Son,

firstborn of all creatures,
begotten of the Father before all ages,

by whom also all things were made;

who for our
salvation
was made flesh and dwelt among
men;
and who suffered and rose again on
the third day,
and ascended to the Father
and shall come again in glory to judge
the living and the dead.
We believe also in one Holy Spirit.

the only-begotten of the Father,
that is, of the substance [*ousia*] of the
Father,
God from God,
light from light,
true God from true God,

begotten, not made, of one substance
[*homoousion*] with the Father,
through whom all things came to be,
those things that are in heaven and those
things that are on earth, who for us men
and for our salvation came down
and was made incarnate and became
man,
suffered, rose again the third day,

ascended into the heavens,
and will come again to judge the living and the dead.
And in the Holy Spirit.

In the first paragraph about God the Father, no disagreement between the two parties is to be found. A comparison of what each says about Christ, however, reveals differences—ones that appear insignificant at first reading, but which represent in fact a watershed between truth and error.

The changes from the first to the second must have rankled the Arians, because it set their course at naught. Rather than the term *Logos* (line 4), the word *Son* is used in the Council's document, strengthened by the modifier *only-begotten*. It emphasizes the likeness of the Son to the Father and stresses the personal nature of their relationship. The Nicene document declares the Son is of the same substance *(or ousia)* as the Father, but Eusebius makes no mention of that concept. Also, instead of "life from life" to describe the Son's coming from the Father (a phrase capable of various interpretations) the much more restrictive "true God from true God" was chosen. The Arian party held

Christ to be not true God, but God in the sense that he is God by grace, and is called God in name only.

Into the Council's creed the term *homoousion* was inserted, an expression from Greek philosophy that is important for what it signifies about the nature of Christ. It can be translated "consubstantial" or "of the same substance," and signifies that the Son and the Father have the same basic nature or essence. The Arians preferred the term *homoiousios*—a word not much different from *homoousion* ("only an iota of difference," as they say)—translated "of similar essence," rather than "of the same essence." This deceptively slight shift makes the Son fundamentally different from the Father.

The use of "came down" in the Nicene Creed implies Christ had been with God before his birth and therefore was not subordinate to him. His humanity was underlined by the addition of "was made man"—not merely "flesh," but "true man."

Appended to the final document of the Nicaea gathering was an anti-Arian anathema:

> But those who say, "There was when the Son of God was not," and "before he was begotten he was not," and that "he came into being from things that are not," or that he is "of a different hypostasis or substance," or that he is "mutable or alterable"—the catholic and apostolic church anathematizes.

Each of these phrases had been used by the Arians to describe the Son. The final anathema concerning the Son's mutability was directed at the Arian belief that, as a creature, Christ was morally changeable, remaining faithful only as an exercise of his will. The council set this view aside, declaring that Christ is of the same invariable substance as his Father, and because of that similarity, unchanging.

When the voices of debate in the council chambers were stilled, and the words were dry upon the parchment, the day of June 19 dawned with eighteen bishops still opposed to the group's consensus. Emperor Constantine then threatened to banish any who refused to sign the creed. Eusebius of Nicomedia and most others finally acquiesced, agreeing to all but the final anathematizing statement. In the end, it was just Arius and two resolute supporters, Bishops Secundus and Theonas, who refused to affix their signatures to any part of the document. True to his word, the emperor deposed the bishops and sent them packing after their leader Arius.

Having concluded their work with a new and, they hoped, unifying creed, the bishops turned their attention to other matters of the church, including the practice of liturgy, the restoration of clerical dignity, the reconciliation of the faithful who had dropped away, the readmission to communion of heretics and schismatics, and the organization of the church. These affairs of discipline occupied them through the hot summer months of July and August, and by August 25 all had been discussed and settled. That day happened to be the twentieth anniversary of the day that Constantine's armies in far-off Britain had elevated him to the position of emperor to succeed his father. The emperor chose to celebrate both that anniversary and the closing of the Council with a grand imperial banquet held at his palace for the bishops, all of whom attended. During the sumptuous meal the emperor showered gifts on those present, ending the Council of Nicaea on a note of joy and celebration.

In the ensuing months, Constantine sent a message to all the churches of his realm, adding his royal weight to the work of the bishops:

> That which has commended itself to the judgment of three hundred bishops cannot be other than the judgment of God, seeing

that the Holy Spirit, dwelling in the minds of persons of such character and dignity, has effectually enlightened them respecting the divine will. Wherefore, let no one vacillate or linger, but let all with alacrity return to the undoubted path of truth, that when I shall arrive among you, which will be as soon as possible, I may with you return due thanks to God, the inspector of all things, for having revealed the pure faith and restored to you that love for which we have prayed.[4]

three

AFTERMATH AND AN ARIAN'S REVENGE

The debates and the outcome of the Council reveal the standards by which the bishops decided what was right and wrong. Their efforts to frame a creed of purely biblical terms demonstrates the importance of the Holy Scriptures as one deposit of truth. A theologian of the previous century had written that faith is buttressed by Holy Scripture, supported by common sense. Athanasius agreed: "The holy and inspired Scriptures are fully sufficient for the proclamation of the truth," adding, "With regard to the divine and saving mysteries of faith, no doctrine, however trivial, may be taught without the backing of the divine Scriptures. . . . Our saving faith derives its force, not from capricious reasonings, but from what may be in the Bible." In the next century, Augustine of Hippo wrote, "In plain teaching of Scripture we find all that concerns our belief and moral conduct."

A second source of truth was the extrabiblical tradition. These were the writings of the church fathers, to which the fathers continually added, and then used as references for guidance and the substantiation of their beliefs. This body of writings was considered an extension of the apostles' teaching, and as such carried their authority. As early as AD 150 it was referred to as "the ecclesiastical canon" and "the canon of faith" by church fathers such as Irenaeus (*c.* 130–*c.* 200), Tertullian (*c.* 160–*c.* 225), Clement of Alexandria (*c.* 150–*c.* 215) and Origen (*c.* 185–*c.* 254).

The liturgy was another treasure for orthodox belief. If something was found in the church's worship, it was considered proper. By the third century the great variety of liturgical practices of earlier centuries was acquiring some fixity. One popular liturgical collection, *The Apostolic Tradition*, viewed the worship of the church as grounded in the apostles and therefore, like the growing extracanonical corpus, enjoying their authority. As we have seen, the catechetical instruction that preceded baptism and the baptismal liturgy were also used by the Council fathers.

When the Nicene Creed was formulated, it was regarded as embodying the truth of these three sources; it was what had been believed from the beginning. In other words, the Council had ratified and passed on the teaching that Christ had given and the apostles had proclaimed.

Despite the establishment of this precedent for the settlement of church disputes, no enduring cessation of conflict flowed from this all-church council.

In truth, it is the witness of history that, despite the councils' contributions to the growing corpus of orthodox faith, and their clarification of issues with the establishment of a consensus, no council has brought lasting peace to the church. Every council has either hardened old divisions or led to new ones. Bringing the adversaries face to face has merely sharpened dissensions rather than healed them.

His imprimatur given to the work of Nicaea notwithstanding, Constantine's faith in the bishops' work began to falter before two years had passed. Perhaps it had been eroded by Eusebius of Nicomedia, bishop of the capital city, related by blood to the imperial family and spiritual advisor to Constantine's half-sister. During the emperor's lifetime, therefore, Arius's friends were able to recover much of the ground they had lost in the council chambers. Eusebius devoted his time to undermining the Nicene bishops, three of whom in particular were well known for their opposition to him.

The first was Eustace, bishop of Antioch. Although orthodox in the faith, he was apparently intemperate of speech: He spoke disrespectfully of Helena, Constantine's mother, calling her a chambermaid while she was on pilgrimage to the Holy Land in 326. At a synod gathered at Antioch he was deposed and banished by her irate son. He never returned, but died in exile in 330.

Eusebius's second target was the star performer in the Nicene drama, Athanasius himself. Athanasius had succeeded to the bishop's chair of Alexandria at Alexander's death in April 328. As he had demonstrated at the Council, he was not afraid to express his opinion or to stand up for what he believed. At one point after the Council he even withstood the emperor. Constantine informed him shortly after his ascension that Arius had finally signed the Creed of Nicaea (with a few private exceptions) and was now to be restored to communion in Alexandria.

Athanasius refused. Summoned before the emperor to make a defense of himself, he so impressed Constantine with his character and dedication that the emperor never forced his hand in the matter.

Despite the steadfast nature of the bishop, however, Eusebius was undaunted in his pursuit of revenge. He had continually lobbied to have Athanasius put out of office, but tripped him up through a minor skirmish at home. As was mentioned in the previous chapter, a group of Christians in Alexandria were adherents of Meletius, a bishop who had declared himself the head of a church composed of a group who had suffered in the persecutions. Meletius had even ordained bishops to serve in his party. Athanasius, their legitimate bishop, had to take action. While this group had agreed to the Council's declarations at Nicaea, they had separated themselves from the organized church. Athanasius did act swiftly, but quite harshly, a fact corroborated by recently discovered papyri, as we have

51

seen. He imprisoned their bishops, refused them the use of churches within his see, and had a number of them beaten.

When the Meletians complained, Eusebius saw his opportunity and struck. A synod called in August 335 was filled with Athanasius's enemies, most of whom had just returned from Jerusalem and the dedication of Constantine's new Church of the Holy Sepulchre in that city. The Eusebian party presented their charges of conduct unbecoming a bishop and petitioned the group for Athanasius's excommunication and dismissal. When the accused arrived with thirty bishops who acted more like thugs than men of God, his cause was not helped. The synod condemned him. Once again, however, he employed his powers of persuasion and obtained exoneration during a personal interview with the emperor.

While this drama was unfolding, a story surfaced about Athanasius's arranging a dock strike in Alexandria that would cut off Constantinople's crucial supply of corn—some 80,000 bushels of grain a day. When Eusebius presented this evidence to the emperor, the latter angrily exiled Athanasius to Trier in Rhineland, Germany, where Athanasius would not know the language and where he would be distant enough to cause no more mischief.

Eusebius's final target was Marcellus, the bishop of Ancyra and a supporter of Athanasius. A relatively obscure figure, Marcellus avoided Eusebius's attention. But once again, it was a trivial, nontheological matter that tripped him up. Constantine wanted a show of unity following the turbulent synod that had ousted Athanasius. He ordered all Eastern bishops to the dedication of his new Church of the Holy Sepulchre in Jerusalem. The significance of the event was heightened by its coincidence with the thirtieth anniversary of his being crowned emperor. As part of the festivities Constantine envisioned a great homecoming and reconciliation for the Arians who had signed the Nicene Creed. Because of his anti-Arian sentiments, Marcellus refused to attend. In 336, at Eusebius's initiative, he was charged with heresy and with disrespect of his emperor. He was subsequently deposed and exiled, surviving the tumultuous years that followed and living until his death at age 90 in 374.

What of Arius, the man who started the whole affair? He had been exiled by Nicaea. His exit from the scene removed him also from the public eye. Time passed. With the three leaders of the Nicene party now removed from the scene, however, he saw an opportunity to return. He traveled to Constantinople and petitioned the emperor for reconciliation with the church. The day before his formal readmission to communion, he was found dead in a public bathroom, the victim of an intestinal hemorrhage. Twenty years after Arius died, his old nemesis, Athanasius, was found telling the story behind his death, according to which the bishop responsible for Arius's reconciliation had prayed that he might not be polluted by his contact with the heretic. The answer to his prayer was supposedly the death of the outcast in a manner similar to that of Judas. Whether the story was true or not no longer mattered, since Arius had ceased to matter. Both sides had moved beyond him. Even his original supporters shunned him, posing their rejection of him in the query, "Why would a group of bishops follow a mere priest?"

Shortly before his death in 337, Constantine was finally baptized into the faith of the church by none other than his longtime advisor, Eusebius of Nicomedia. He was laid in state in the white robe of a newly born believer, and buried by his son Constantius in his new Church of the Holy Apostles in Constantinople, the city named for him. He was succeeded by his three sons—Constantine II, Constans, and Constantius—who divided the empire among themselves.

With the passing of the first Christian emperor, the initial post-Nicene controversy was at an end.

four

THE DEATH OF
ARIANISM

With Constantine's death came also the death of the truce among his three sons. Although they had agreed to parcel out the empire among themselves, after their father's death war broke out between Constantine II and Constans. Constans not only defeated his older brother, but executed him and annexed his provinces. From 340 on, therefore, he was sole ruler of the West. His brother Constantius remained the sovereign of the East.

With a new order in place, Athanasius returned to Alexandria and sought once again to rally the bishops to the creed of the Nicene Council. His old enemy, Eusebius of Nicomedia, however, also had moved—to Constantinople, now the effective capital of the East, where he was made bishop. In that same year the followers of Eusebius consecrated a certain Gregory as bishop of Alexandria, even though the other bishops of Egypt had formally declared their support of Athanasius. With an armed guard and a city terrorized by the show of force, Gregory installed himself as bishop in Athanasius's place.

Athanasius fled Alexandria, escaping westward to Rome at the invitation of Pope Julius (337–352), and there he joined Marcellus and other pro-Nicene exiles. The following year Julius assembled a synod that exonerated both Athanasius (finding his conduct blameless and reinstating him as bishop of Alexandria) and Marcellus (declaring him of sound orthodox belief). The pope then wrote a formal letter to the East asking why he had not been informed of the proceedings in Alexandria, as custom dictated, and informing the bishops there that any charges against the bishop of that city should have been sent to him as the bishop of Rome. The letter was a sign of the growing power the pope wielded as bishop of Rome. The church in the East never responded.

This exchange between the East and the West was typical of the disparity between the two parts of the church. Socrates (380–450), a church historian of these years, writes of the communication:

> The situation was like a battle by night, for both parties seemed to be in the dark about the grounds on which they were hurling abuse at each other. Those who objected to the term *homoousios* imagined that its adherents were bringing in the doctrine of Sabellius and the Montanists [two heresies], so they called them blasphemers on the ground that they were under-

mining the personal subsistence of the Son of God. On the other hand, the protagonists of *homoousios* concluded that their opponents were introducing polytheism, and steered clear of them as importers of paganism. . . . Thus, while both affirmed . . . [many of the same doctrines about the Son and the Father], they were somehow incapable of reaching agreement, and for this reason could not bear to lay down arms.

The divisions within the church troubled many. On January 6, 341, ninety-seven Eastern bishops sat with Constantius in official convocation in Antioch, grieved over the bitter dissension. In a move toward reconciliation with the West, these church leaders, who had had quarrels with those supporting the creed developed by the Council of Nicaea, divorced themselves from Arius and declared that their only opposition to the creed was its lack of clarity to exclude obvious heretics, such as Marcellus. They were unable to agree, however, with Rome's claim that it was a court of appeal for the whole church, since they considered it a new thing for a Western synod to judge decisions made in the East. While they maintained that the Roman church certainly possessed the tradition of apostolic doctrine, they reminded them that it was from the Greek East that the apostles had first traveled to Rome!

The proceedings at Antioch illustrate the gravity and complexity of the Arian controversy. It was no longer an abstract and remote dispute about the theses of a slightly neurotic and popular preacher in Alexandria. A real split between East and West was imminent. Besides resentment over the Roman claim to superior jurisdiction over Eastern affairs, the Eastern church looked down on the intellectual abilities of their Western colleagues. For their part, the West thought the Greeks too subtle and clever. Further confounding their attempts at reconciliation was the difference in the languages they spoke. When Greek was translated into Latin, the terms did not match up one-for-one, and the waters of debate were consequently muddied. In addition, having the Arian Eusebius of Nicomedia as spokesman for the Eastern church made it difficult for Rome to believe that the Greek bishops were not Arians, despite their claims to the contrary.

Matters were deadlocked until the death of Eusebius in the winter of 341–42 left the Eusebian party without a leader. By this time, as we have seen, Constantius had become the sole emperor in the East. When a joint appeal came to him from both his bishops and Julius of Rome, he convened a council of both East and West to discuss the conflict. Assembling the following year at Sardica (later Sofia), the Eastern bishops walked out even before it began, because they saw Athanasius and Marcellus, their enemies, being seated. They also may have been afraid of being outvoted, since they knew a majority was against them.

The synod subsequently split into two camps, each roundly cursing the other. The threat of schism was momentarily realized. The separated councils, however, did not waste all their time hurling epithets at one another. At length the East produced a creed with an anti-Arian anathema, and the West published a weak theological statement justifying their decision to admit Marcellus of Ancyra to communion. Eventually the East agreed to take back Athanasius at Alexandria— a concession to the West; and the West silently dropped the cause of Marcellus— a concession to the East.

In 346 Athanasius reentered Alexandria to an enthusiastic welcome. Civil officials journeyed a hundred miles into the desert to meet him, and Alexandria's citizenry poured out of the city like a river to surround him and welcome him home. For the next ten years

Athanasius enjoyed his longest single period of uninterrupted ministry. Four hundred bishops from every corner of the empire declared themselves in communion with him. The long-standing schism that had occasioned the Council in Nicaea seemed healed at last.

It was four years later, however, that Constans, the Western emperor and supporter of the Nicene party, died. A usurper, Magnentius, was declared emperor during a rebellion that followed, but Constantius of the East refused to recognize him. A bloody civil war ensued, and Constantius won a decisive victory over Magnentius, establishing himself as the sole sovereign of the reunited empire. During his reign the Arians enjoyed once again their moment in the sun, founded as it was upon the emperor's power and person. Their triumph proved short-lived, however, because in 361 he too died.

In the following years the persuasions of the emperors continued to govern the tide of the battle within church and empire. New theological positions were staked out, and new warriors stepped up to take the place of those who had died. During these years, Athanasius continued to exert influence in the fray. He had changed—no longer a zealot, he was now an elder statesman whose authority had been established by his singleminded devotion to orthodoxy. He found himself sought out for advice by younger theologians and church figures who needed his seasoned point of view in their continuing struggles. He died in 373, perhaps the last survivor of those who had been present at Nicaea a half-century earlier.

Five years after the death of Athanasius, in August 378 the reigning emperor Valens was killed in a battle against the Goths. His successor, who had been raised in Spain by parents sympathetic with the pro-Nicene outlook of the Western bishops, was Theodosius. The Nicene party was about to rise again!

The new emperor sent advance warning to the East that he would recognize only those bishops and churches that accepted the Nicene Creed and were in communion with the pope in Rome. Two years later he stepped directly into the scuffle, condemning the Arians and enjoining upon his empire the faith that "the Apostle Peter had taught in days of old to the Romans, and which was now followed by the pope Damasus and by Peter, [then] bishop of Alexandria, a man of apostolic sanctity." Those who opposed him were heretics, denied the name "catholic," and forbidden the right of assembly.

In the capital of Constantinople, parishes held by Arians were confiscated and their bishop deposed. Gregory Nazianzus, a strong spokesman for the Nicene point of view, was installed as the new bishop, as the emperor looked on approvingly. The moment seemed graced by heaven when a brilliant shaft of sunlight suddenly broke into the darkened basilica, illumining all within.

When Gregory was later disqualified on a technicality, Nectarius, an elderly civil official taken from the imperial legal department on the recommendation of the emperor, was installed in his place. He was so free of past association with any party in the controversy that he had not even been baptized. He was rushed through the sacrament and consecrated bishop in his baptismal robes (not an unheard-of practice)!

To further consolidate the Nicene victory, Theodosius summoned to Constantinople, his capital city, a regional council of Eastern bishops in May 381. Of the 150 attending, no Western figures were invited, although one was there by oversight. A creed that bears the name of this Council of Constantinople falls solidly within the tradition of Nicaea, but scholars today doubt that it was produced by them. Whatever its origin, it emerged from a conference in 451, the Council of Chalcedon, as the official creed of the whole church of Christ.

Curiously enough, it has subsequently been given the name "Nicene Creed," and it is by this title that we know and recite it today. While this creed is very close to that produced by the Council of Nicaea, viewing them side by side makes the changes evident:

The Creed of the Council of Nicaea

We believe in one God,
    the Father, the Almighty,
    maker
    of all that is, seen and unseen

We believe in one Lord, Jesus Christ,
    the Son of God,
    begotten of the Father as Only-
        begotten,
    that is, from the substance of the
        Father,
    God from God, Light from Light,
    true God from true God,
    begotten, not made,
    of one Being [*homoousios*] with
        the Father.
    Through him all things were made,
    things in heaven and things on
        earth.
    For us and for our salvation
        he came down:

he became incarnate

The "Nicene Creed"

We believe in one God,
  the Father, the Almighty,
  maker of heaven and earth,
  of all that is, seen and unseen.

We believe in one Lord, Jesus Christ,
  the only Son of God,
  eternally begotten of the Father,

God from God, Light from Light,
true God from true God,
begotten, not made,
of one Being [*homoousios*] with
    the Father.
Through him all things were made.

For us and for our salvation
  he came down from heaven:
by the power of the Holy Spirit
    he became incarnate from the

and was made man

and suffered.

On the third day he rose again;

he ascended into heaven.

He will come again to judge the
living and the dead.

We believe in the Holy Spirit.

Virgin Mary,
and was made man.
For our sake he was crucified
    under Pontius Pilate;
    he suffered death and was
    buried.
On the third day he rose again
    in accordance with the
    Scriptures;
he ascended into heaven
And is seated at the right hand of
    the Father.
He will come again in glory to
    judge the living and the dead,
    and his kingdom will have no
    end.

We believe in the Holy Spirit, the Lord, the
    giver of life,
    who proceeds from the Father.
    With the Father and the Son he is
    worshiped and glorified.
    He has spoken through the Prophets.
    We believe in one holy catholic and
    apostolic church.

We acknowledge one baptism for the
forgiveness of sins.
We look for the resurrection of the
dead,
and the life of the world to come.
Amen.

The "Nicene Creed" as we have it
today is somewhat different from the
creed of the Council of the same name.
The first paragraph of each, concerning
God the Father, is similar, since a consensus about the Father's role as Creator had
been reached and affirmed at Nicaea.

The second section deals with the Son
and is in both creeds a buttress against
the entry into the church of Arian errors
about the nature of Christ. Although the
explanation "from the substance of the
Father," is missing from the second, we
do find preserved the Nicene byword,
homoousios (translated, "of one Being").
The phrase "his kingdom shall have no
end" was included to deny a heresy
developed by an old friend of the pro-

Nicene group, Marcellus of Ancyra (d. 374), who claimed that the Word was just a temporary projection of the Father's energy, not in any way equal with him. Although Christ had been sent by God for the redemption of humankind, his body would be reabsorbed into the Father at the Last Judgment! It is easy to see why his cause was dropped by the West.

In the third section that concerns the Holy Spirit, we find a cautiously worded statement that reflects the reasoning of a leading bishop of the day, Basil of Caesarea. Basil recognized that the church's liturgy treats the Holy Spirit in the same manner as the Father and the Son. In the *Gloria Patri,* he noted, their equality is clearly stated: "Glory be to the Father and to the Son and to the Holy Ghost [Spirit]." Also, in the formula used in baptism similar words are said: "in the name of the Father and the Son and the Holy Spirit." This equal standing is included in the second creed: "With the

Father and the Son he [the Spirit] is worshiped and glorified." They are worshiped in unity, but are distinct from one another. While both Son and Spirit find their origin in the Father, the Son is *"begotten* of the Father," while the Holy Spirit *"proceeds* from the Father."

One contribution the Council of Constantinople made to this final creed come at the instigation of Emperor Theodosius, who was ever interested in unifying his empire. The council chose phrases from Scripture, rather than terms of philosophy, to describe the third member of the Trinity. These were more widely accepted and easier to understand. Calling the Holy Spirit "Lord" is based on Paul's description, "Now the Lord is the Spirit, and where the Spirit of the Lord is, there is freedom" (2 Corin. 3:17). Describing him as "life-giver" comes from Jesus' teaching: "It is the spirit that gives life" (John 6:63), as well as from Paul's words, ". . . the letter kills, but the Spirit gives life" (2 Corin. 3:6).

That he proceeds from the Father is taken from Jesus' own description: "the Spirit of truth who comes from the Father" (John 15:26), a verb the bishops seized upon. The Spirit's inspiration of the prophets is ascertained from 2 Peter 1:21: ". . . no prophecy ever came by human will, but men and women moved by the Holy Spirit spoke from God."

Beliefs about the church, baptism, the resurrection of the dead, and eternal life, absent from the original, were included in the second creed.

The doctrinal decisions of the Council of Constantinople marked the end of the Arian attempt to capture the church of the empire. Their beliefs lived on only among the Goths, converted as they had been by Arian missionaries. Within the empire itself Arianism died unloved and unlamented.

five

THE CREED
FOR TODAY

Although centuries have passed since the Nicene Creed was written, and most of the figures in the drama of its creation have been forgotten, the truths to which it witnesses have changed not at all. The God the Nicene fathers worshiped remains unchanged; the life his Son died and rose to give as a blessing to God's sons and daughters is still being offered. The story of Jesus' life has been told in more languages than one might count, and untold billions have responded to his invitation to have life and have it abundantly (John 10:10). It therefore seems appropriate to close this little book on the Creed for today with a look at its significance for life in the twenty-first century.

> *We believe in one God,*
> *the Father, the Almighty,*
> *maker of heaven and earth,*
> *of all that is, seen and unseen.*

The creed produced by the Council meeting at Nicaea began with the singular pronoun *I,* because it had originated with a confession of faith uttered by a single candidate at the time of baptism. When recited today in a church setting, however, the Creed becomes corporate and appropriately begins with *We.*

The Latin verb for "to believe," *credere,* has as its root the word *cor,* meaning "heart," plus an old verb, *do,* meaning "to put, to place, or to set." Our word "credit" has the same origin. Believing in something, therefore, is more than giving a casual nod of affirmation—it means committing oneself, giving one's heart to the object of faith.

The first affirmation of belief concerns God. The belief in one divine Being is the foundation of all monotheistic religions. To believe in one God is to say there is only one ultimate Reality. Christians trace this belief to their spiritual forebears, the Jews, whose fundamental tenet is summed up in the *Shema:* "Hear, O Israel: the LORD is our God, the LORD alone" (Deut. 6:4). Jews, Christians, and Muslims alike affirm that God is a divine being greater than any other—good or evil, imaginary or real.

The Council affirmed that this divine power is called "Father," based on Jesus' calling him that. Humans strive to bridge the great gap between the known and the Unknown by using terms that are familiar, and this is an example. When we speak of God as "Father," therefore, we mean, "God is *like* a father." To call God by this name is for Christians to affirm his relationship with his Son, Jesus Christ, as well as with us, his sons and daughters on earth. *Father* also means God is personal, not just a gigantic force. Chance and luck may be blind, but he is not. The Council made no effort at this point to define what God is in himself, but rather who he is in his relationship to humanity.

Some have objected to describing God in male terms, saying that such words are a sexist way of referring to the Eternal One, who is above maleness and femaleness. It is true that God encompasses traits traditionally assigned to both genders. God is a protector, an initiator, a source of strength; he is constant and undaunted. He is also a nurturer, a consoler, an intimate friend; he is compassionate, understanding, and merciful. Whatever we need, God is. Efforts to find a term other than "Father" that connotes both the parenting and the life-generating activities of God have, in the opinion of this writer, proven unsuccessful. This is true as well of the search for a gender-inclusive pronoun: hence the use of "he" in references to the Divine in this book.

The creed also asserts that God is *almighty*. He has power and authority—he is bigger, mightier, and prior to all else. This characteristic of God may stand in tension with our calling him "Father." While the latter word connotes familiarity and accessibility, the former conjures images of transcendence and majesty. God revealed himself to Moses as "I AM WHO I AM" (Exod. 3:13–15), a self-sufficient being, existing in himself. There is nothing he cannot handle, and he has no worries. For us harried humans, this can be a boon. Before we bring him a problem, he knows the answer. His omnipotence means he has no trouble communicating with us.

Besides his power, the term "almighty" also embraces his holiness. He is "other" than we. The Bible is full of references to the holiness and otherness of God. The halls of heaven resound with the seraphim's unending song: "Holy, holy, holy, the Lord God the Almighty" (Rev. 4:8). When God appeared to Moses in the bush that burned without being consumed, he was told to remove his sandals because he walked on "holy ground" (Exod. 3:5). At the giving of the Ten Commandments, Sinai shook with earthquake, lightning, and fire because God had descended there (Exod. 19:16–20). Many pious Jews today will not even utter his name, but write it with four unpronounceable consonants: *YHWH*. Mere humans may not approach this holy God without adequate preparation. The wonder of it all is that One as holy as he is so "down to earth," so immanent and personal.

God's might also signifies his omnipresence. He is present both here where I am and there where you are. He resides in the past, in our present, and in the future, all at the same time. He is always everywhere. He can heal our past, comfort us now, and take care of our future. He never sleeps. His faithfulness is from everlasting to everlasting.

The creed not only asserts God's fatherhood and might, but it also declares him *Creator*. "In the beginning God created the heavens and the earth" (Gen. 1:1) is the grand proclamation that opens the Bible. As the originator of all of reality, he has made all that is, what we see and what we cannot see. Everything would cease to exist (an incomprehensible idea) if God ceased to exist (an even more absurd thought!). All that is owes its being to God.

> *We believe in one Lord, Jesus Christ,*
> *the only Son of God,*
> *eternally begotten of the Father,*
> *God from God, Light from Light,*
> *true God from true God,*
> *begotten, not made,*
> *of one Being with the Father.*
> *Through him all things were made.*

With these words, the second and principal section of the creed begins. Peter declared to the crowd gathered some fifty days after Jesus' resurrection, "Therefore let the entire house of Israel know with certainty that God has made him both Lord and Messiah, this Jesus whom you crucified" (Acts 2:36). *"Kyrios Christos"* (Greek for "Christ is Lord") is the earliest known confession of faith in this man from Nazareth. The New Testament Scriptures refer to Jesus as "Christ Jesus" or "Jesus the Christ," "Christ" meaning "Messiah." In a world electrified by the expectation that God would send a divine figure to free Israel from Roman domination, Jesus' miraculous career made many think he was that one who would free the nation from all her enemies and inaugurate the final age of supremacy for her and peace for the world. While it was natural for his disciples and others to refer to him as *Messiah,* he redefined the meaning of the term, dying and rising to establish, not a political, but a spiritual kingdom. References to him by this title entered the church's earliest baptismal confessions of faith, as well as later affirmations such as the Nicene Creed, becoming a part of the church's vocabulary ever since.

The Creed states that all things were made through him. The Gospel of John makes the same proclamation: "All things came into being through him, and without him not one thing came into being" (1:3). The Apostle Paul echoes the idea that Christ was the channel of creation, and crowns his acclamation by adding that he was the objective for which all was created: "He is the image of the invisible God, the firstborn of all creation; for in him all things in heaven and on earth were created, things visible and invisible . . . —all things have been created through him and for him" (Col. 1:15–16). Paul also observes that the Son is the "cosmic glue" that bonds all of creation: "in him all things hold together" (Col. 1:17).

> *For us and for our salvation*
> *   he came down from heaven:*
> *by the power of the Holy Spirit*
> *   he became incarnate from the*
> *   Virgin Mary,*
> *and was made man.*

With these words, the Creed begins a description of Jesus that deals with you and me. His life with his Father *before* Bethlehem is affirmed—"he came down from heaven"—as is his miraculous birth through the agency of the Holy Spirit. Termed the "incarnation," this God-become-human action of the divine is stated succinctly by John: "The Word became flesh and lived among us" (1:14). For the men who drafted the Nicene Creed, this was much more than a philosophical proposition; it was a matter of life and death.

Every religion seeks to solve the mystery of evil in the world, and for every diagnosis there is a matching remedy. Christianity is no different. The Bible traces evil to the beginning of time, to the Garden of Eden. As stated in the old adage, "In Adam's fall, we sinned all," the Christian faith holds that in that primordial paradise, humanity lost its relationship with God, along with any claim to eternal life. In the disobedience of Eve and Adam, the union of man and woman was ruptured, as was their relation with the animal kingdom and the world around them. (Read the account in Genesis 2:4b–3:19.) It is hard to dispute the reality that we are a "fallen" people; the evidence is all about us—and also within, to the honest observer.

The framers of the creed viewed Jesus' incarnation as God's answer to humanity's dilemma. To carry our burden, he became human; to save us, he remained fully God. While the first half of the Father's answer was his Son becoming human, the second was his death and resurrection:

> For our sake he was crucified under
> Pontius Pilate;
> he suffered death and was buried.
> On the third day he rose again
> in accordance with the Scriptures;
> he ascended into heaven
> and is seated at the right hand of
> the Father.

He will come again in glory to judge
the living and the dead,
and his kingdom will have no end.

When the fathers formulated the Creed, they portrayed Jesus' crucifixion and death as being "for our sake," as Scripture affirms. Without consulting us, Christ unilaterally suffered and died and rose for all humankind. Because the disobedience of our first parents ruptured all our relationships, God acted in his Son to restore us, first in relationship with himself, and then to one another and to the world around us.

While many good people have died for what they believe, Jesus Christ was more than a martyr. He was the Son of God. Three days after his burial—much against anyone's expectations—he returned to life! God was well pleased with his Son. It quickly became a cornerstone of the new faith, that this definitive act of the Father was absolutely essential to the truth of that new faith. The

Apostle Paul said everything else depends on it:

> . . . if Christ has not been raised, then our proclamation has been in vain and your faith has been in vain. If Christ has not been raised, your faith is futile and you are still in your sins. If for this life only we have hoped in Christ, we are of all people most to be pitied. (1 Corin. 15:14, 17, 19)

Without this objective and supernatural action, the Christian faith may be little more than a cult following a teacher who did good for others, fell afoul of his enemies, and was killed for what he believed.

The Christian church believes that not only did Christ rise from the dead, but also he returned to his Father in heaven, to the exalted state he possessed before his descent to earth.

But there is more. As the angels told the disciples as they gazed into the sky into which Jesus had just disappeared, "Men of Galilee, why do you stand looking up toward heaven? This Jesus, who has been taken up from you into heaven, will come in the same way as you saw him go into heaven" (Acts 1:11). The details of this "Second Coming" have been debated since before the New Testament was written, yet the truth remains. As the Son came once in humility to be born of woman, the church longs for his return in glory. His advent will signal the end of life as we know it. This life of sin, pain, and suffering, of joy, accomplishment, and waiting, will be no more. Something too wonderful for words will supersede it.

What we await is rooted in the very nature of God. Doubtless it will include reunion with those we have loved long since and lost for a while (as Cardinal Newman said). It will be the consummation of every longing of the human heart, the fulfillment of our fondest dreams. The creed calls this future "his kingdom," and it will last forever. Because a kingdom is the place where a sovereign reigns, we can envision transpiring there only what God wills to happen, not as it is in this present age, where his perfect will is hampered by sin.

> *We believe in the Holy Spirit, the*
> *Lord, the giver of life,*
> *who proceeds from the Father*
> *and the Son.*
> *With the Father and the Son he is*
> *worshiped and glorified.*
> *He has spoken through the*
> *prophets.*

Before they had formed any notion of the Holy Spirit, the early Christians felt the force of this third Person of the Trinity. Fifty days after the resurrection (on the day of Pentecost) the followers of Christ were praying together, when they suddenly heard and felt a blast of air and saw fire that did not burn—signs they understood as the Holy Spirit come among them. (Read the account in Acts 2:1–4.) Those who had witnessed the resurrected Christ were suddenly filled with his Spirit, the Spirit of God—as have all believers since that great day. He had been sent from heaven, sent to give life to all who believe in the Son of God.

The second phrase—"who proceeds from the Father and the Son"—looks innocent enough; but it has been the cause of church division, which the Council had set out to heal. It was not originally part of the Creed, the one agreed to by the East and West, but was inserted around the year 600, and afterward, in versions of the affirmation used by the Western church. There was no malice in this move. The addition of the words "and the Son" grew out of popular practice in a time when the church was seeking to affirm the equality between the Father and the Son, counteracting vestiges of Arian thought that still lingered in pockets of the faithful. (Despite all the work that went into fashioning the Nicene Creed, Arian thought flared up now and again throughout the

Christian church.) This addition of "and the Son" concurred with Scripture—Jesus describes the Spirit as the one "whom *I* will send to you from the Father, the Spirit of truth who comes from the Father" (John 15:26; emphasis added)—but the Eastern church clung tenaciously to the original text as agreed upon in the ecumenical councils. During subsequent clashes between East and West, this short addition, termed the *filioque* ("and the Son") clause, remained one of the insuperable barriers dividing the church of Christ. Negotiations between Rome and Constantinople have sought to resolve the conflict, but to date no resolution has been found.

> *We believe in one holy catholic*
> *and apostolic church.*
> *We acknowledge one baptism for*
> *the forgiveness of sins.*
> *We look for the resurrection of*
> *the dead,*
> *and the life of the world to come.*
> *Amen.*

In this concluding section the Creed draws to a rapid close with four additional elements affirming essential aspects of the Christian faith. The first statement is often misunderstood. Many Protestants refuse to use the word "catholic"—using instead the term "universal"—because they believe it refers to the Roman Catholic Church. Given the historic animosity between Protestants and Catholics, such a negative attitude, while not laudable, is understandable. The Creed, however, predates any formal divisions in the church, and these adjectives describing the church refer to the entire fellowship of the faithful.

The term "holy" first appeared in the second century and has been used since. It is a reference, not just to the people, but also to God as Lord of the church. The old testament refers to the "holy people" of God four times, and such a description was easy to apply to those who followed Jesus Christ.

"Catholic" means simply "universal." Whether a particular tenet of faith is universal is a test of whether it is correct belief. Defined by the fifth century monk, Vincent of Lérins, the term "catholic" means simply "what has been believed everywhere, always, and by all."[5] The word is inclusive, embracing the faithful of all centuries, living throughout the world.

"Apostolic" alludes to the apostles, generally regarded as the twelve disciples of Jesus, including Matthias, picked to replace Judas, who had betrayed Jesus, and also including the missionary Paul. The original twelve are viewed as the foundation of the church: the men Christ personally chose, who lived and traveled with him, who grieved his death and witnessed him risen from the grave. As we have seen in the formation of the Creed, an appeal to the apostles or to their writings often settled a doctrinal matter and silenced opponents. Truth had been passed from Christ to them, and subsequently to the church.

The second tenet of faith involves baptism. Following the example of Christ's immersion in the Jordan, as well as his mandate to baptize all people in his name (Matt. 28:19), a rite of initiation with water has admitted newcomers to the church from the beginning. Water is an appropriate substance for this ceremony; just as it washes away external dirt in bathing, in baptism it removes the pollution of sin. Encounters with water have marked God's dealings with his human family since the Great Flood (Gen. 6:11–9:29). Perhaps the most dramatic event was the crossing of the Red Sea (Exod. 14), an event that reverberates throughout the Old Testament and is alluded to by writers of the New Testament. The dramatic change from the old life to the new that Christ gives us is described by Paul: "If anyone is in Christ, there is a new creation: everything old has passed away; see, everything has become new!" (2 Corin. 5:17). The striking transformation is enacted in baptisms performed in a stream or a river. The candidates enter the moving water, are three times immersed (in the name of the Father, the Son, and the Holy Spirit), and exit the stream by the opposite bank, a symbolic passing from the old life, through cleansing, and into the new.

If baptism begins life in the church, the resurrection of the dead will begin life in heaven. This element of faith has been included in creeds since the second century, affirming the goodness of creation, over against the gnostic belief that physical matter is inherently evil and therefore irredeemable. When the Lord Christ returns to earth at the end of time, all who have died since the beginning of time will come to life. This is a mystery according to the Bible (1 Corin. 15:51), beyond human understanding or explanation. It begins "life in the world to come," the new and eternal age of peace, for which humankind has longed. Old and New Testament seers foretold the wonders of this reign of God. To the seventh-century-BC prophet Isaiah, this time will be one when "the wolf shall live with the lamb," and "they will not hurt or destroy on all [God's] holy mountain; for the earth will be full of the knowledge of the LORD as the waters cover the sea" (Isa. 11:6, 9). The lonely exile on the island of Patmos, the writer of the book of Revelation, wrote down his vision of the end: "Then I saw a new heaven and a new earth; for the first heaven and the first earth had passed away, and the sea was no more. And I saw the holy city, the new Jerusalem, coming down out of heaven from God. . . . I saw no temple in the city, for its temple is the Lord God the Almighty and the Lamb [i.e., Jesus]. And the city has no need of sun or moon to shine on it, for the glory of God is its light, and its lamp is the Lamb" (Rev. 21:1–2, 22–23).

We have come full circle in our consideration of the Nicene Creed. As it was

God the Father who created all that is, it is he who brings his creation to its perfect and full end. The curse that humanity brought on itself at the beginning has been lifted. God the Father's will, thwarted in Eden, caused Jesus Christ his Son to come and fulfill that will, providing the way to life with God forever, for all who choose to believe.

NOTES

1   R.P.C. Hanson, *The Search for the Christian Doctrine of God* (Edinburgh: T & T Clark, 1988) p. 253.

2   Henry Bettenson, editor and translator, *The Early Christian Fathers* (London: Oxford University Press, 1956) p. 396.

3   Philip Schaff and Henry Wace, editors, *Nicene and Post-Nicene Fathers*, Second Series, Volume I (Grand Rapids, Michigan: Wm. B. Eerdmans Publishing Co., 1984).

4   Schaff and Wace, *Nicene and Post-Nicene Fathers*, Chapter 9.

5 Schaff and Wace, *Nicene and Post-Nicene Fathers*, "The Commonitory," Chapter 2.

GLOSSARY OF TERMS

one God there is only one ultimate and supreme power of the universe.

the Father, the Almighty two characteristics of God, who is both parent and omnipotent.

heaven and earth comprising all that exists—seen and unseen, known and unknown.

Jesus *Savior* in Hebrew; the name of Mary's son, given to Joseph by an angel (Matthew 1:21).

Christ *anointed* or *messiah* in Greek; it places Jesus as the ultimate and fulfilment of the long line of kings (made so by a ritual of anointing [smearing] with oil) who ruled God's people.

begotten   in contradistinction to *created*. Christ is not part of creation.

true God from true God   Christ is completely divine.

of one Being with the Father   In his most fundamental nature, Christ is exactly like God the Father.

Through him [Christ] all things were made God created all things by means of Christ (John 1:3).

salvation   Scripture describes humankind as lost, in need of rescue (Romans 5:12–14).

by the power of the Holy Spirit   by means of, by the agency of, the third member of the Trinity, three unified, equal and divine persons, Father, Son and Spirit

he became incarnate   Christ was conceived, became human.

from the Virgin Mary   Mary's conception of her son, Jesus, was supernatural, after which she remained a virgin

crucified   affixed to a cross, a Roman instrument of torture.

Pontius Pilate the governor put in power by the Romans, who ruled the region where Jesus lived. Under Pilate's direction Christ was put to death.

he suffered death and was buried a cardinal Christian belief, that the Son of God physically died.

On the third day   three days after Christ was killed; i.e. on Sunday.

he rose again   another seminal article of faith, that God raised his Son to life from the grave.

ascended into heaven Christ returned to his Father when his work on earth had been completed.

the right hand of the Father   At the king's right hand was the place of supreme honor.

to judge the living and the dead Scripture asserts that at the end of time Christ will return to earth and judge all who have died and all who are alive at his return.

the Holy Spirit the third member of the Godhead, sent by the Father and the Son to give life to those who believe in Christ.

the giver of life the Spirit gives both physical and spiritual life.

catholic universal (not a particular reference to the Roman Catholic Church)

apostolic related to the 12 apostles, whom Christ commissioned to start the church.

one baptism for the forgiveness of sins By means of baptism our faults are pardoned.

the resurrection of the dead When Christ returns at the end of time, all who have died will come to life.

the life of the world to come The faithful will live forever with God in heaven.